OUT OF THE MIST

A COLLECTION OF LYRICS AND POEMS

BY

MATTHEW KUSHI

Thank you to all of my friends and family who have encouraged me and given me feedback. When I write, there is a story to tell, an emotion to convey and a message to show. These can be stand alone or set to music. When I write, I usually have a tone, a cadence or melody that guides the style and flow of the piece, hence why these are called lyrics and poetry.
~Matthew Kushi

Matt Kushi is from Hadley, MA. He is a writer, an agricultural business owner and an agricultural/athletics/ education technician. He enjoys writing and "painting with words."

TABLE OF CONTENTS

A Love Discovered

There was a man and a woman,
Friends with wild dreams in a small town.
She was smart and beautiful;
He was honest and hard-working,
With a shy streak to match.

She saw him laugh
And be the charm of everyone's life.
But she didn't know the half
Because she never saw the longing eyes
Or the silent tears that he held inside.

He said,

I am right here
Just waiting for you, my Dear.
I see you dancing with this and that one.
I know that I could love you good and love you right,
You are the one that I hold dear.
So, if you see me,
I am standing right here.

Always there for each other,
They were as close as could be.
Someone to talk to and a shoulder to cry upon,
It seemed like a story from long ago.
Some nights he lies awake dreaming and thinking

I am right here
Just waiting for you, my Dear.
I see you dancing with this and that one.
I know that I could love you good and love you right,
You are the one that I hold dear.
So, if you see me,
I am standing right here.

The key is still in the lock,
It just needs someone to dare to enter and open.
And there they may find what one has been hoping;
A love, a friendship forever unlocked and discovered
By two hearts that saw each other.

A War Letter
© 2016 Matthew Kushi

I saw you before I left that night.
We have known each other for so long
But we barely know each other.
I noticed that talking to you in the fading light.

I'm going somewhere far away.
Don't know if and when I'll be back.
Hopefully someday rather than never.
I'm scared and I've got no one to write to.

Would you let me write to you?

I hope that you can read this letter.
I'd type it if I could but for now my hand will have to do.
It's a whole other world over here.
I hope that you are able to read this letter
And I hope that you decide to write back.
The thought of your words brings a sliver of light to my hurting heart.

There is something about this place that doesn't make sense;
There is something about this whole situation that isn't right.
There is a war raging on that drives us to insanity.
If I am able to return back, I hope that it is all of me.

I hope that you are reading this letter
And I am dreaming that you care enough to write back.
Or, at least, I am hoping that you are reading the words I am writing.
A man gets mighty lonesome in a world like this.

So many of us doing our duty.
Don't know what this place will leave of me.
We all have each other out here
But we all know that we can't replace home or you, my dear.

I hope that you can read this letter.
I'd type it if I could but for now my hand will have to do.
It's a whole other world over here.
I hope that you are reading this letter
And I hope that you decide to write back.

In my mind, I've learned to love you
And when I get back, I'll do right by you.
I dream that you will be proud to have me.
For now, the thought of your words is enough to comfort me.

Dear Elloise

Dear Elloise,
A raindrop falls but the storm passes.
And a rainbow forms
And shines down on your bright new face.
And the cry rings down the hall,
Welcome to this world, dear Elloise.

The stars and the dawn
Welcome you, dear Elloise.
Open your eyes and take in this world,
It's such a beauty to see.

You were born in July
And soon you will see why
This world can be such a special place.
The sky paints colors of gold;
There are so many stories for you to be told.
In time you will see, dear Elloise.

Your future is a blank canvas
Waiting for you to swirl and twirl it with your colors.
I hope that you learn to love and love to laugh.
Without joy, our worlds are only half.
Live, laugh, learn and be inspired all you please,
Dear Elloise.

Though young, you can probably tell
Your parents will guide you well.
You have entered a world that is full of joy and beauty,
When we pull back the curtain and allow ourselves to see.
This will all come to you in time,
Dear Elloise.

The stars and the dawn
Welcome you, dear Elloise.
Open your eyes and take in this world,
It's such a beauty to see.
In time, you will see.
I welcome you to this world,
Dear Elloise.

Ellis Island
© *2016 Matthew Kushi*

I have left my land of old
And set sail upon the blue seas
To begin a new story that has yet to be told.
I gaze upon the twi-lighting horizon
With a feeling of fear and hope.

They call it the island of hope and the island of sorrow.
I don't know which it will be until tomorrow.
I will work hard for our dreams to come true.
Hope you believe me as I look at you.

I am heading to the land called Ellis Isle,
Leaving the old and starting anew,
Nothing with me but the clothes on my back and you.
It won't be easy but it can't be harder than what my eyes have seen.
The dawn is breaking on a new day of our lives
As we head to America and Ellis Island.

At last I can see land,
See the waves breaking onto the sand.
Our new home this will be.
Good times are coming, hopefully.
Wait and see…

I am heading to Ellis Isle
And starting anew.
Take in the beauty of this new land
As we pull into America and Ellis Island.

Our new age has finally begun.
Honor the old ways but let the hard times be done.
It doesn't matter your name,
You can try to build your American dream just the same
Once we are able to pass through Ellis Island.

I Know That It Hurts

© 2016 Matthew Kushi

Tears falling down on your heart,
I can see into your eyes.
You are cold and shivering from a cold rain;
You're trying to hide the pain.
My heart feels shattered and it's not even mine.
Hang on, don't let this tear you apart.

I know that it hurts.
A broken heart does, I know.
But baby, please don't give up.
You are something special.
I don't know if you will hear my words,
But I am here for you.

I may not be much,
But, darling, if you can see through your tears
You will see me waiting for you.
Go ahead and cry, I'm on your side.
Please let me hold you in my arms.
All I want to do is to see you smile.

Thunder and lightning go hand in hand
And with you, I am willing to make my stand.
Let me embrace you in my arms as I fall into yours.
When this storm has passed,
I hope we have opened instead of closed doors.
I don't expect your broken heart to heal.
That's alright, there is time.
But I hope when the time comes, it is me you feel.

I know that it hurts right now.
Darling, let me pull you close;
I am here for you.
Close your eyes and let yourself go.
I've realized that I love you more than you can know.
I know that it hurts
But please let me hold you in my arms
And show you how much I care.

If I Asked You To Stay

You told me that you needed to leave,
To get away from here.
You said that you weren't sure if there was a future here.
I could see the pain of those words in the dawning eve.

I nodded and wished you well.
Told you that I would sure miss you.
Later that night, as I thought of your words,
I thought of what I could do.

If I asked you to stay,
Would you not go away?
I truly want to see you be happy
But I don't want you to leave.
If I asked you to stay,
Would you not go away?
Would you stay?

I don't know if your future is with me.
I don't know what the future holds at all.
But I know that you mean more to me
Than you realize. More than I realized.
I've just been too afraid to let you see.

I don't know why
But you can make a day bright
Just like a day warmed by the newborn light.
The thought of you leaving brings a tear to my eye.
The more I think of you, the more I realize
I'm not ready to say good-bye.

When I talk to you

If I asked you to stay,
Would you not go away?
I truly want to see you be happy
But I don't want you to leave.
If I asked you to stay,
Would not go away?
Would you stay?

Just To Be With You
© *2016 Matthew Kushi*

Working hard in the fields,
My head doesn't sing a song of melody;
It sings a song to the vision of you.
Don't know why I do, but I think of you.

You've got a way,
As the stories of old say,
That makes a man lose himself
Inside of a heart of gold.

When I look into your eyes,
I wish that I could know what you see.
I would give anything to know what you are thinking
And what secrets you are holding inside of your heart.
You fascinate me
You move me.
I wish that I could know what you really see,
What you really think of me.

Don't want to spend another minute of my life without you;
Take my hand
And take me with you.
I want to see
What kind of fire that a spark from love can do.
Though we already share so much,
I want you to know
That I'd walk through that fire with you.
Just to be with you.
I only want to be with you.

Saw you hurt once,
Don't ever want to see that again.
Not because it made you weak;
It made you stronger.
Seeing someone you care about hurt is the worst pain for a friend.

Don't want to spend another minute of my life without you;
Take my hand
And take me with you.
I want to see
What kind of fire that a spark from love can do.
Though we already share so much,
I want you to know
That I'd walk through that fire with you.
Just to be with you.
I only want to be with you.

My Darling
© 2015 Matthew Kushi

I've been walking in circles,
Just trying to think it all out.
Our world's were so close at the start.
Now it seems like there are mountains driving us apart.

I guess that we stayed too long.
I kept hoping that things would change.
But every day, I came home to the same song.
We were just too distant, Too far gone.

I look in the mirror
And try to see the man that I was.
Am I so different?
Or was fate telling us that we were fooling ourselves.

I see your vision during the day
I see you at night
Oh…my darling
I want to hold you so tight
Oh…my darling
With you, I was right
Oh…my darling
Oh…my darling.

When the story is all told and done
And we can turn the pages of us,
We will find that it was neither of us.
I loved you before and I love you now,
There's no reason to figure out why or how.

I see your vision during the day
I see you at night
Oh…my darling
I want to hold you so tight
Oh…my darling
With you, I was right
Oh…my darling
Oh…my darling.

I see your vision during the day
I see you at night
Oh…my darling
I want to hold you so tight
Oh…my darling
With you, I was right
Oh…my darling
Oh…my darling.

New England Dairy
© 2016 Matthew Kushi

Looking out on lush fields of green,
The Dairy Farmer surveys his hay and corn.
"Hope it rains soon", the man with a hard face says.
If it doesn't rain soon, the crop may be gone.

What's the price of milk today?
The old countertop refrain.
It's holding steady but looks like it could drop.

Up every morning when the stars meet the rise of day,
The dark blue screen opens its doors
And lets in the white cloud and light blue sky.
Sure looks like a good day to cut some hay.
This life of dairy farming is hard work
but I wouldn't have it any other way.

What's the price of milk today?
The sky turns cloudy
And the rain comes down on me.
As the man on the radio says,
Hard times are a-coming,
That price is starting to drop.

Bruised hands and sore back,
Been milking all day
But she doesn't complain.
Looks over at her son and daughter
Rationing out the water
And a smile begins to come across her face.

What's the price of milk today?
Better fix the leak
Because it's still dropping.

Heading to the office today,
We're a proud New England Dairy Family
But I don't know what to say.
Got to keep the kids in school
And give everyone in the family a reason to smile.
He's read the latest story from the A.P.
And it wasn't kind to the dairy program of MPP.
"Don't know but I hope that my Uncle Sam can help me,
As a New England Dairy Farm Family is what we were meant to be
And it means all the world to me."

What's the price of milk today?
Maybe tomorrow the folks will be saying
That the corn is good and the weather is fit for haying
And that the hundredweight price of milk is rising.

Out Of The Mist
© 2016 Matthew Kushi

Out of the mist
At the dusk of night and the dawn of a dream,
I saw you in a vision.
You reached out and told that all would be alright.
Then, like the breeze, you were once again a memory.
When will you appear again,
Out of the mist?

Born to a farmer
And raised by the land,
His hands were made strong and his heart bold
By the life of the farm.
His passage began by tending the cows and the crops with
The heart of a boy on a journey of a man.

Never had fame, never had want and was guided by the light.
He knew his place
And he knew wrong from right.
All the fame and want he needed in life
Came to him from the love of his kids and his wife.
Making a living and working the fields brought a smile to his face.

He gave and taught love;
Worked hard up until the end.
An honest, small town man living his life in the right.
But one day in May,
The heart that had worked and loved so much,
Was suddenly called to up Above.

His time was too short.
When he comes to visit,
Time doesn't seem to exist.
Please don't go, I wish that you could stay.
I wish that you weren't gone and could remain
Out of the mist.

Out of the mist,
Gone too soon.
Wish you could come back and stay awhile.
Oh, we loved you so much and we miss you.
Please don't be a stranger
And visit again
Out of the mist.

Sealed In A Bottle
© 2016 Matthew Kushi

When you are down, I stand up for you.
I will stand out in a crowd for you to lean on me.
Sometimes I wonder what people think of me.
I wonder if they know that I am stronger than I seem.
Or do they not even see me?
You see,
I care for others
But I want someone special to care about me.

Sometimes I need someone too…

You may notice me staring into space
But no one knows what I am thinking.
People don't read my face...
I wish you would.

You may notice a crack in my voice
But I then quickly turn away.
I don't let you see the tears in my eyes.
I don't give you a chance to ask if I'm fine
So I don't tell you all of my lies.
I swallow hard and seal it away.

Too many times I take my feelings and store them away.
I don't let people see
The real me.
I don't know why I do it.
Don't know why I cry.
But I take all of the joy and hurt
And seal it in a bottle.
Seal it like a letter in a bottle.

I hide behind a caring smile
And try to make everyone else smile for awhile.
Even in pain, you will never know I am hurt
Until you see me collapse and hit the dirt.

I bottle my emotions up and seal them in a bottle.
Pick me up and throw me away deep into the sea,
One day I hope someone opens it and feels the real me.
But I know it starts with me…

Too many times I take my feelings and store them away.
I don't let people see
The real me.
I don't know why I do it.
Don't know why I cry.
But I take all of the joy and hurt
And seal it in a bottle.
Seal it like a letter in a bottle.

Blue Sky
© *2016 Matthew Kushi*

There is a story that is as old as time
That the older you get, the wiser you get.
It is also said that the older you get, the more innocence you lose.
Easy as it may be to walk that road,
It depends on what you choose.

When my time's are dark and cloudy, I look to the skies
And in the blanket of nightfall I think of this daytime scene.

I think of a blue sky so high and crisp
I think of a brown field of freshly turned dirt ready for planting
And the clear water of river that is in no hurry to end its journey.
At that moment, only the current time is what matters
As I dream of blue sky, brown fields and clear waters.

Life can be stoic
And you can become callous before you know it.
But don't forget to smell the roses and the rain
And all of the good things in this life that make you sane.

Everyone's got their own world in which they can escape.
When you come from a valley of fields and open sky,
It really is not too hard to understand why
My most pleasant memories come from nature's landscape.

When my times are dark and cloudy, I look to the skies
And in the blanket of nightfall I think of this daytime scene.

I think of a blue sky so high and crisp.
I think of a brown field of freshly turned dirt ready for planting
And the clear water of river that is in no hurry to end its journey.
At that moment, only the current time is what matters
As I dream of blue sky, brown fields and clear waters.